Want to Go Out for a Bite?

by Tim Harrod

Andrews McMeel
Publishing

Want to Go Out for a Bite?

Marv Albert's Favorite Pick-up Line and Other Jokes from the Headlines

Want to Go Out for a Bite? copyright © 1998 by Tim Harrod. All rights reserved. Printed in the United States of America. No part of this book may be used or reproduced in any manner whatsoever without written permission except in the case of reprints in the context of reviews. For information, write Andrews McMeel Publishing, an Andrews McMeel Universal company, 4520 Main Street, Kansas City, Missouri 64111.

www.andrewsmcmeel.com

98 99 00 01 02 BIN 10 9 8 7 6 5 4 3 2 1

Library of Congress Cataloging-in-Publication Data
Harrod, Tim
    Want to go out for a bite? : Marv Albert's favorite pick-up line and other jokes from the headlines / Tim Harrod.
       p. cm.
   ISBN: 0-8362-5194-6 (pbk.)
   1. American wit and humor.   I. Title.
PN6162.H354 1998
818' .540208—DC21   97-40939
                                                                                    CIP

Design and composition by Mauna Eichner

ATTENTION: SCHOOLS AND BUSINESSES

Andrews McMeel books are available at quantity discounts with bulk purchase for educational, business, or sales promotional use. For information, please write to: Special Sales Department, Andrews McMeel Publishing, 4520 Main Street, Kansas City, Missouri 64111.

Contents

General	1
Clinton/Gore	35
Princess Diana	103
Politics/General	113
Mother Teresa	139
Michael Jackson	145
O.J. Simpson	165
John Denver	185
Sports	203

Bill Gates/Microsoft	221
Heaven's Gate	257
Ellen DeGeneres	275
High-Tech	283
The Unabomber	297
Versace	303
Marv Albert	311
Kelly Flinn	319
Mike Tyson/Evander Holyfield	325

General

To celebrate the McVeigh verdict Denny's restaurant is offering a new breakfast special: *They take white bread and fry it.*

A New York toy company has begun marketing "Billy," the first-ever gay doll.

               Other than Ken.

Q: Why was baby Jesus born in a stable?

A: His parents were in an HMO.

Q: How many gangsta rappers are there in the country?

A: Depends if you ask me now or ten minutes from now.

Hot on the heels of Dr. Kevorkian's album of jazz compositions is the announcement that he'll be touring the country performing. His stage name for his musical career is DeathRow Tull. And his first album is "Unplugged."

Q: Why would Eddie Murphy make a lousy farmer?

A: When he picks up a hoe he doesn't do anything with it.

Q: Why would Frank Gifford make a great farmer?

A: See above.

Q: Why don't they make white M&Ms?

A: Because they'd enslave the brown M&Ms, steal all the red M&Ms' land, accuse the yellow M&Ms of obstructing trade, and complain that the damn coffee M&Ms were taking all their jobs.

Q: Why was America so stunned by the Donald Trump/Marla Maples divorce?

A: If any two things go together, it's maples and rich sap.

McDonald's canceled the fifty-five-cent price on Big Macs and other sandwiches, citing confusion by the public and franchises. After the Arch Deluxe debacle and now this, McDonald's has begun placing tote boards outside listing the number of marketing ploys the public didn't buy so far this year.

Q: How do you get a nun pregnant?

A: Dress her as an altar boy.

A couple, both sixty-seven years old, went to the doctor's office. The doctor asked, "What can I do for you?" The man said, "Will you watch us have sexual intercourse?" The doctor looked puzzled but agreed. When the couple had finished, the doctor said, "There is nothing wrong with the way you have intercourse," and he charged them $20. This happened several weeks in a row. The couple would make an appointment, have intercourse, pay the doctor, and leave. Finally the doctor asked, "Just exactly what are you trying to find out?" The old man said, "We're not trying to find out anything. She's married and we can't go to her house. I'm married and we can't go to my house. Holiday Inn charges $32. Hilton Hotel charges $37. We do it here for $20 and I get $18 back from Medicare for a visit to the doctor's office."

Q: How successful was McDonald's fifty-five-cent Big Mac promotion?

A: Ronald McDonald recently spent a night in the Lincoln Bedroom.

Hot on the heels of the blockbuster Tickle Me Elmo doll, Mattel has come out with their own doll—Fondle-Me-Barbie.

Mattel is also introducing "Divorced Barbie"—it comes with half of Ken's stuff.

GENERAL

Q: What do you call a transvestite in Ebonics?

A: Susan B. Anthony.

Q: Why were there only forty-nine contestants in the Miss Ebonics U.S.A. Pageant?

A: Nobody wanted to wear the sash that said "Idaho."

Q: How do you use the word "before" in ebonics?

A: 2 + 2 before.

Ebonics Exam:
Use each of the following words in a sentence.

1. **Hotel**—I gave my girlfriend crabs and the hotel everybody.

2. **Rectum**—I had two Cadillacs, but my ol' lady rectum both.

3. **Disappointment**—My parole officer tol' me if I miss disappointment they gonna send me back to the big house.

4. **Foreclose**—If I pay alimony this month, I'll have no money foreclose.

5. **Catacomb**—Don King was at the fight the other night. Man, somebody give that catacomb.

6. **Penis**—I went to da doctor and he handed me a cup and said penis.

7. **Israel**—Alonso tried to sell me a Rolex, I said, "Man, that looks fake." He said, "No, Israel."

GENERAL

8. **Undermine**—There is a fine lookin' ho livin' in the apartment undermine.

9. **Tripoli**—I was gonna buy my old lady a bra but I couldn't find no tripoli.

10. **Stain**—My mother-in-law axed if I was stain for dinner again.

11. **Seldom**—My cousin gave me two tickets to the Knicks game, so I seldom.

12. **Odyssey**—I told my bro, you odyssey the tits on this ho.

13. **Horde**—My sister got into trouble because she horde around in school.

14. **Income**—I just got in bed wit dis ho and income my wife.

15. **Fortify**—I axed da ho how much? And she say fortify.

WANT TO GO OUT FOR A BITE?

America Online has promised refunds to subscribers unable to connect via overloaded phone lines. The bad news is, to get the refund, subscribers must go to http://www.aol.com.

Q: Why did God invent the cockroach?

A: So the paparazzi could have someone to look down on.

Q: What is the difference between leeches and the paparazzi?

A: Leeches fall off after you die.

WANT TO GO OUT FOR A BITE?

Q: Did you know that Oscar Mayer has selected a new kid to be the company's commercial spokesman?

A: They picked Jeffrey Dahmer, the only man in America whose bologna really did have a first name!

GENERAL

The government released its final report claiming that the Roswell, New Mexico, aliens were in fact dummies. As evidence they point out that they went to New Mexico in the summer.

If the best gift one can receive is something that a child has made, does that mean that the best gift to buy is anything from the Kathie Lee Gifford clothing collection?

GENERAL

Q: Did you hear about the Canadian who won a gold medal at the Olympics?

A: He was so proud of it that he brought it home and had it bronzed.

Six reasons computers must be female:

1. As soon as you get one, a better one is just around the corner.

2. No one but their creator understands their internal logic.

3. Even your smallest mistakes are immediately committed to memory for future reference.

4. The native language used to communicate with other computers is incomprehensible to everyone else.

GENERAL

5. The message "Bad command or filename" is about as informative as: "If you don't know why I'm mad at you, then I'm certainly not going to tell you."

6. As soon as you make a commitment to one, you find yourself spending half your paycheck on accessories for it.

Q: Why was the cloning of a sheep by Scottish scientists so surprising?

A: Because Scots have been fooling around with sheep for years, but it's the first time one ever got pregnant.

Q: Did you know they're making a movie about the Grand Forks flood?

A: It's called *A River Runs Over It*.

Q: What's the difference between the old army and the new army?

A: In the old army men got blown *out of* the foxholes.

Garry Kasparov, the chess master, has a plan to reclaim his title. He's going to schedule the rematch with the computer for just after midnight, January 1, 2000.

Q: What does it mean when the flag at the post office is flying at half-mast?

A: Now hiring!

Two hundred Southern Baptists were stranded on Treasure Island in Disneyland Sunday night. They refused to take the ferry.

GENERAL

> Now the Southern Baptists are boycotting *The Flintstones*. They absolutely refuse to have a gay old time.

The nineteen shortest books in the world:

19. *Al Gore: The Wild Years*

18. *Amelia Earhart's Guide to the Pacific Ocean*

17. *America's Most Popular Lawyers*

16. *Career Opportunities for History Majors*

15. *Detroit—A Travel Guide*

14. *Different Ways to Spell "Bob"*

13. *Dr. Kevorkian's Collection of Motivational Speeches*

12. *Easy UNIX*

11. *Ethiopian Tips on World Dominance*

10. *Everything Men Know about Women*

GENERAL

9. *Everything Women Know about Men*

8. *French Hospitality*

7. *George Foreman's Big Book of Baby Names*

6. *How to Sustain a Musical Career* by Art Garfunkel

5. *Mike Tyson's Guide to Dating Etiquette*

4. *One Hundred and One Spotted Owl Recipes* by the EPA

3. *Staple Your Way to Success*

2. *The Amish Phone Book*

1. *The Engineer's Guide to Fashion*

NASA has developed a new strategy to counter critics who say that the agency spends too much and doesn't provide sufficient direct benefit to the average taxpayer: They're going to publish a series of instructional books based on their unique R&D experience! The first title is expected to be *Repairing and Upgrading Orbital Radiotelescopes for Dummies.*

Clinton/ Gore

They say the women in Arkansas are so fast that they have to put a governor on them!

Arkansas is very proud of Clinton—all these women coming forward and none of them are his sister!

At the beginning of his first term, Clinton called the White House interior decorator into the Oval Office. He was furious and said, "Chelsea is very upset because she thinks she has the ugliest room in the entire White House; I want something done about it immediately!" "Yes Sir, Mr. President," the interior decorator replied. "I'll take those mirrors out right away!"

WANT TO GO OUT FOR A BITE?

Bill Clinton is a president for our times, a truly composite commander in chief. He has the hormones of John F. Kennedy, the scruples of Richard Nixon, and the memory of Ronald Reagan.

Ever since he met JFK, Clinton wanted to be president in the worst possible way... now he's succeeding beyond his wildest dreams.

WANT TO GO OUT FOR A BITE?

If character is not an issue, why isn't Ted Kennedy president?

What did Ted Kennedy
have that Bill Clinton
wished he had?
 A dead girlfriend.

Q: Have you heard about the new Bill Clinton doll?

A: You pull the string and it never tells the same story twice.

Q: What was Bill Clinton's favorite part of the Olympics?

A: The Opening Ceremonies, because it was the only time he could be around an old flame and not have to dodge allegations.

President Clinton was addressing the media. When asked about Whitewater, he replied: "Will you people just get off the Whitewater thing, it's ancient history!" To which Bob Dole responded: "Hey, you leave me out of this!"

Bill Clinton was walking along the beach when he stumbled upon a genie's lamp. He rubbed it, and lo and behold a genie appeared. Bill was amazed and asked if he got three wishes. The genie said, "Nope...due to inflation, I can grant you only one wish. What'll it be?" Bill didn't hesitate. He said, "I want peace in the Middle East. See this map? I want these countries to stop fighting with each other." The genie exclaimed, "Gadzooks, man! These countries have been at war for thousands of years. I'm good, but not *that* good. I don't think it can be done. So make another wish." Bill thought for a minute and said, "You know, people really don't like my wife. They think she's a real bitch and ugly as sin. I wish for her to be the most beautiful woman in the world and I want everybody to like her." The genie said, "Lemme see that map again."

Q: What's the difference between President Hoover and President Clinton?

A: One promises a "pig in every pot," the other is a pig who smokes pot.

Q: When did Clinton first regret being a draft dodger?

A: After reading about the Tailhook investigation.

Over five thousand years ago, Moses said to the children of Israel, "Pick up your shovels, mount your asses and camels, and I will lead you to the Promised Land." Nearly five thousand years later, Roosevelt said, "Lay down your shovels, sit on your asses, and light up a Camel. This is the Promised Land." Now, Bill Clinton is going to steal your shovels, kick your asses, raise the price of Camels, and mortgage the Promised Land.

You may have read in the news that President Clinton has banned the use of federal funds in research of cloning humans. He has a political motive in doing this: as it is always easier to clone the lower forms of life, it will allow the Republicans to become a majority by the next election!

President Clinton comes back from a weekend trip to Arkansas. He gets off Air Force One with a pig under one arm. The Marine Corp Sergeant salutes and says, "Sir, welcome home, sir! That's a nice pig, sir!" President Clinton is very indignant and says, "Soldier, this is no pig, this is a genuine Arkansas Razorback Hog." The Sergeant says, "I'm sorry, sir. That's one fine hog, sir." President Clinton says, "I got it for Hillary." The Sergeant says, "Good trade, sir!"

WANT TO GO OUT FOR A BITE?

The title for Hillary Clinton's next book will be *It Takes a Village to Keep an Eye on My Husband.*

The Clintons are at an Orioles game when a secret service agent whispers something into the president's ear. Bill gets up and drags Hillary out of the stadium and then returns to his seat like nothing happened. The secret service agent comes back and tells the president, "You misunderstood me. They wanted you to throw out the first pitch."

Chrysler Corporation is adding a new car to its line to honor Bill Clinton. The Dodge Draft will begin production in Canada this year.

Q: Did you hear that President Clinton has started a National Registry of Sex Offenders?

A: His little black book was full.

Q: What is the difference between Clinton and the *Titanic*?

A: Less than 1,000 women went down on the *Titanic*.

Gennifer Flowers reassures us that the White House budget is fine. In her experience, the president already has a very small staff.

Bill Clinton has been mistakenly characterized as a "yes man" when he is really a "yes ma'am."

Asked about his views on euthanasia, Clinton replied, "Youth in Asia are just like kids everywhere else."

The Clintons are at a restaurant. The waiter tells them the day's specials are chicken almondine and fresh fish. Hillary orders the chicken.

The waiter asks, "And the vegetable?"

"Oh, he'll have the fish," Hillary replies.

WANT TO GO OUT FOR A BITE?

Q: What do Gennifer Flowers and John Huang have in common?

A: They both helped with the presidential erection.

Q: How can you pick President Clinton out at the Olympics?

A: He'll be the only American there rooting for the Russians.

Clinton is out jogging. He passes a young boy selling puppies.

"Buy a puppy, sir?" asks the lad.

"Oh, no, sorry," says Clinton. "We have a puppy and a cat already, you know."

"But they are Democratic puppies, sir," asserts the enterprising lad.

Clinton smiles, but again declines. The boy nods, Clinton jogs on.

The next day Clinton is jogging by the same spot. There again is the boy, still trying to sell the puppies.

As Clinton jogs by he overhears the youth telling a potential customer, "But sir, these are Republican puppies."

Clinton stops and says, "Young man, yesterday you told me those were Democratic puppies."

"Well sir," explains the child, "since then their eyes have opened."

President Clinton commenced the first round of White House staff cuts. It is reportedly the first time Mr. Clinton has given a woman a pink slip that he hasn't asked her to try on first.

Clinton and Gore were discussing premarital sex. Al asked Bill, "I never slept with my wife before we were married, did you?" Bill replied, "I'm not sure, what was Tipper's maiden name?"

Q: What advice did Clinton give Frank Gifford?

A: "Next time, send your people ahead to do an electronic sweep of the area."

Q: Why do people take an instant dislike to Hillary Clinton?

A: It saves time.

Q: What do you get when you cross a crooked politician with a dishonest lawyer?

A: Chelsea.

Like all fathers, President Clinton was saddened by his daughter's leaving home to go off to college. But the president noted that there is a bright side: "At least I'll have another room to rent out."

Q: Did you hear that Bill Clinton recently attended an auto show?

A: The fine print in the ad said, "All models available."

Q: How can you tell that the guy who attacked the White House with a plane was insane?

A: He seems to have thought Clinton would be in his own bedroom at night.

Clinton, Dole, and Perot are on a long flight in Air Force One. Perot pulls out a $100 bill and says, "I'm going to throw this $100 bill out and make someone down below happy." Dole, not wanting to be outdone, says, "If that was my $100 bill, I would split it into two $50 bills and make two people down below happy." Of course Clinton doesn't want these two candidates to outdo him, so he pipes in, "I would take one hundred $1 bills and throw them out to make one hundred people just a little happier." At this point the pilot, who has overheard all this bragging and can't stand it anymore, comes out and says, "I think I'll throw all three of you out of this plane and make 250 million people happy."

Clinton and Gore are jogging one day, and Bill says to Al, "When I get home I think I'm going to rip Hillary's panties right off!" Al says, "I didn't know jogging got you so excited." Bill says, "Oh, it's not that, it's just that they're riding a bit high."

Rush Limbaugh and Hillary Clinton were riding in an elevator together. Hillary pressed the "STOP" button, ripped off her clothes, and said, "Oh, Rush! Make me feel like a woman!" Rush ripped off his clothes and said, "Okay! Fold these!"

A recent poll of 200 women asked the question, "Would you sleep with Bill Clinton?"

94% responded, "Never again."

In a related story, a truck bomb scare in the front driveway of the White House resulted in the evacuation of the building, until Secret Service agents ascertained that the Ryder van parked in the drive was just the Gores waiting out front with their furniture.

Did you hear about the new bonds issued by the Clinton administration?

The Stephanopoulos bond never matures, the Gore bond has no interest, and the Clinton bond has no principle.

Q: Bill and Hillary are on a sinking boat. Who gets saved?

A: The nation.

Q: Did you hear that at Clinton's fiftieth birthday party his cake was made in the shape of the United States of America and decorated with the fifty states?

A: It was similar to the one Dole had on his fiftieth birthday, which was decorated with the thirteen colonies!

An international group of doctors was at a convention in Switzerland. The topic of discussion was the new medical technology from their respective countries.

A German doctor said, "In my country, medicine is so advanced, we can perform heart surgery on a person on Monday, and have him back to work in two weeks."

Then a Japanese doctor said, "That's nothing! We can perform an appendectomy on a person on Tuesday, and have him back to work by Saturday."

An American doctor said, "That's nothing! We can take an asshole from Arkansas, put him in the White House, and half of the country is out of work the next day!"

Someone is marketing Bill Clinton golf balls. They don't fly straight but they sure give you a great lie.

What's Al Gore's advice to Bill Clinton?
   TAKE A SKI VACATION!

Clinton is out cruising one evening and spots a hooker on the corner.

He stops and asks her, "How much?"

"One hundred," says the hooker.

Bill checks his pockets and says, "All I got is a twenty."

"No way," says the hooker. "You can't get hardly anything for twenty."

Bill goes on his way. Later that night Bill and Hillary go out to dinner. On their way into the restaurant the same hooker walks by. She looks at Bill and Hillary and says, "See, I told you that you can't get much for twenty bucks!"

CLINTON/GORE

Al Gore is a true legend. Everywhere he goes, there is a statue personifying him.

Chelsea asked her dad, "Do all fairy tales begin with 'Once upon a time'?" Bill Clinton replied, "No. Some begin with 'After I'm elected.'"

President Clinton will be starring in his own TV show next season. It's called *Welcome Back Carter.*

Did you hear it took three secret service agents to hold Hillary's hand down during the swearing-in ceremony?

If the Clintons divorce before 2001, who will get the house?

Hillary and Donna Shalala, Secretary of Health and Human Services, are such feminists that they insisted on the removal of balls from the White House pool table.

When Clinton was asked about *Roe vs. Wade*, he replied, "I think the Haitians had better row because it is too deep to wade."

WANT TO GO OUT FOR A BITE?

Clinton's mother prayed fervently that Bill would grow up and be president.
So far, half of her prayer has been answered.

Isn't putting Bill Clinton in charge of a trust fund a bit illogical? You know, like making a draft-dodger commander in chief?

When Clinton was asked what he thought about foreign affairs, he replied, "I don't know. I never had one."

Think about the position Al Gore is in: just a heartbeat away from the vice-presidency.

WANT TO GO OUT FOR A BITE?

The good news about Clinton's health care plan is that everyone will be covered. The bad news is that it will be with dirt.

If you came across Bill Clinton struggling in a raging river and you had a choice between rescuing him or getting a Pulitzer Prize–winning photograph, what shutter speed would you use?

A guy goes into the saloon in a little town in Montana. He has a few beers and then he says, "Clinton is a horse's ass"—and the guy standing next to him bashes him in the head. After he recovers from that and has a few more, he says, "Clinton and his boss Hillary are both horses' asses!" Several people give him dirty looks, and the two nearest guys beat the shit out of him. A few minutes later, he recovers, looks around the room and yells, "I still say Clinton is a horse's ass!!" Everybody in the place jumps him, and he is beaten to a pulp. Hours later, he wakes up and everyone is gone except for the bartender. "Wow," the guy says, "This is a really Democratic town." The bartender says, "There wasn't a Democrat in the house—they're all horse ranchers."

If Clinton wanted legislation to burn down the Capitol building, Republicans in the Senate would introduce a compromise bill to burn it down over three years.

One day God was looking over creation and He decided that He wasn't really happy with the way things turned out. So He called the three most powerful men on Earth—Bill Clinton, Boris Yeltsin, and Bill Gates—to come and see Him. He told them that this experiment with life on Earth was a failure, and that in three days He was going to end it. So basically, they had three days to prepare their people.

Boris Yeltsin convened an emergency meeting of the Russian Supreme Soviet and said: "I have bad news, and really bad news. First of all, there is a God. Second, everything we have worked for since the revolution will be totally destroyed in three days."

Bill Clinton called a press conference and said: "I have good news and bad news. First of all, there is a God. Second, everything we have worked for since the Revolution will be destroyed in three days."

Bill Gates convened a meeting of the board of directors and said: "I have good news, and really good news. First of all, there is a God. Second, in three days, IBM will be destroyed."

WANT TO GO OUT FOR A BITE?

A man went to heaven and saw clocks everywhere. There were grandfather clocks, wall clocks, watches, and alarm clocks in every corner. It appeared that heaven was nothing more than a giant clock warehouse. The man asked St. Peter, "What's the deal? Why are all these clocks here in heaven?" St. Peter replied, "There is one clock for each person on Earth. Every time the person tells a lie, his clock moves one minute. For instance, this clock is for Sam, the used-car salesman. He must be close to finalizing a deal with a customer right now," said St. Peter. "The minute hand on his clock moves all day." The man and St. Peter next saw a clock with cobwebs on the minute hand. "Whose clock is this?" asked the man. "That clock belongs to the Widow Mary. She is one of the finest, God-fearing people on Earth. I bet her clock hasn't moved in a year or two." After a complete tour of heaven, the man said, "I've seen everyone's clock but President Clinton's. Where is his clock?" St. Peter said, "Just look up. We use it for a ceiling fan."

Socks the White House cat is a neutered male. That makes *two* guys in the White House who don't have any balls!

Bill Clinton's popularity has been declining so much that even Paula Jones is claiming she never met him!

WANT TO GO OUT FOR A BITE?

The first couple were driving through Little Rock, and they passed by a gas station. A big man yelled, "Hi Hillary!" and Hillary said, "Hi Bubba!" Bill asked who Bubba was. Hillary told him he was an old high school boyfriend, and Bill said, "If you had married him you would be married to a gas station attendant, but you married *me* and now you're the first lady." And Hillary told him, "If I had married him he'd be the president and you'd be the gas station attendant."

Q: What did Bill Clinton do after the first abortion bill crossed his desk?

A: He paid it!

Q: Did you hear that President Clinton was out for his morning jog when someone threw a beer at him?

A: It was a draft, so he dodged it!

Q: Why is President Clinton usually in a bad mood?

A: P.M.S.

Q: What happens when you wind up the Hillary Clinton doll?

A: It winds up the Bill Clinton doll.

Q: What happens when you wind up the Gennifer Flowers doll?

A: It unwinds the Bill Clinton doll.

Princess Diana

Q: What's the difference between Dodi Fayed and Tiger Woods?

A: Tiger has a good driver.

This deadly crash is just another example of the Franco/German anti-British collaboration that has been going on since 1914. Surely it's no coincidence that the world's best-loved Englishwoman was killed by a drunken Frenchman driving a German tank.

Q: What's the one word that could have saved Princess Diana's life?

A: Taxi.

Q: Why wouldn't you want to buy any computer hardware at Harrods?

A: Their drivers are crash-prone!

Q: Have you heard that the Ritz is looking for a new driver?

A: They want one with tunnel vision.

If Teddy Kennedy
had been driving,
they would have
taken the bridge.

PRINCESS DIANA

Q: What did the Queen say when she heard that Princess Diana had died in a car crash?

A: "Was Fergie with her?"

Q: What's the difference between the London Ritz and the Paris Ritz?

A: You get mints after dinner at the London Ritz, and minced after dinner at the Paris Ritz.

Q: What did Princess Di say to Dodi after he gave her the ring?

A: Aren't we moving a bit too fast?!

Q: What did Dodi say to his chauffeur?

A: "Wanna go to Paris with me and Di?"

Q: What do Diana and Versace have in common?

A: They both got screwed by queens and died.

Just before the accident, the chauffeur shouted, "We're going to die, we're going to die!" To which Dodi replied, "No, we're going to my place."

Q: Did you hear about the new Bruce Willis movie?

A: It's going to be called *Di Hard* or *Live and Let Di* or *One Wedding and a Funeral*, and it's to be shown only in drive-in theaters.

Politics/ General

Congressmen are like diapers— they need to be changed frequently, and for the same reason.

Q: Did you hear that the Democrats and Republicans are finally, once and for all, going to balance the budget?

A: Well, I know it's not funny, but it sure is a joke.

POLITICS/GENERAL

The two U.S. cities with the highest alcohol consumption are Las Vegas and Washington, D.C. The difference between the two is that in Washington the drunks are gambling with *our* money!

Saddam Hussein is visiting a school. In one class, he asks the students if anyone can give him an example of a tragedy.

One little boy stands up and offers this explanation: "If my best friend who lives next door was playing in the street when a car came along and killed him, that would be a tragedy."

"No," Hussein says. "That would be an 'accident.'"

A girl raises her hand and offers this definition: "If a school bus carrying fifty Iraqi children drove off a cliff, killing everyone involved, that would be a tragedy."

"I'm afraid not," explains Hussein. "That is what we would call a 'great loss.'"

POLITICS/GENERAL

The room is silent and none of the other children volunteer. "What?" asks Hussein. "Isn't there anyone here who can give me an example of a tragedy?"

Finally, a boy in the back raises his hand. In a timid voice, he speaks: "If an airplane carrying Yassar Arafat, Colonel Kaddafi, and Saddam Hussein were blown up by a bomb, *that* would be a tragedy."

"Wonderful!" Hussein beams. "Marvelous! And can you tell me *why* that would be a tragedy?"

"Well," says the boy, "because it wouldn't be an accident, and it certainly would be no great loss!"

WANT TO GO OUT FOR A BITE?

The House of Representatives voted overwhelmingly to approve the reprimand of Newt Gingrich for ethics violations. The reprimand includes a reimbursement of $300,000. Currently, the House is debating Gingrich's request to pay using a check drawn from the House bank.

Q: What is twelve inches long and hangs in front of an ass?

A: Gingrich's tie.

WANT TO GO OUT FOR A BITE?

Rush Limbaugh and his chauffeur were out driving in the country and accidentally hit and killed a pig that had wandered out on a country road. Limbaugh told the chauffeur to drive up to the farm and apologize to the farmer.

They drove up to the farm, the chauffeur got out and knocked on the front door, and was let in. He was in there for what seemed like hours. When he came out, Limbaugh asked the driver why he had been there so long.

"Well, first the farmer shook my hand, then he offered me a beer. Then his wife brought me some cookies, and his daughter showered me with kisses," explained the driver.

"What did you tell the farmer?" Limbaugh asked.

The chauffeur replied, "I told him that I was Rush Limbaugh's driver and I'd just killed the pig."

POLITICS/GENERAL

General Motors is installing radios in all its cars with the dial stuck on Rush Limbaugh's show. It's the cheapest way to install an airbag in a car!

Physicists discovered a new element that is the heaviest known to man. It is white and acidic, instantly polarizes all elements that come into contact with it, and emits heat but no light. They promptly voted to name it Limbaughium.

POLITICS / GENERAL

Q: What do you call Newt Gingrich and Bob Dole sitting in the front seats of your car?

A: Dual airbags.

Q: If Newt Gingrich, Bob Dole, and Rush Limbaugh jumped off the World Trade Center, who would hit first?

A: Who cares?

Q: Newt Gingrich, Bob Dole, and Jesse Helms are all alone on a deserted island. Who survives?

A: We do!

Q: Why is Rush Limbaugh's show like PBS's *Barney & Friends*?

A: Both feature a bunch of intellectually underdeveloped fans fawning over a big, fat, shallow puppet.

Q: On which vehicle are you most likely to see a RUSH IS RIGHT bumper sticker?

A: The one blowing the most smoke.

POLITICS/GENERAL

Bob Dole was at a press conference and someone asked him, "So, Mr. Dole, which is it—boxers or briefs?"

He said, "Depends!"

Q: Where does Rush Limbaugh recruit his studio audience?

A: From *Amazing Discoveries*. They'll applaud car wax.

Q: If you were in a room with Hitler, Mussolini, and Rush, and you only had two bullets in your gun, what should you do?

A: Shoot Rush twice!

POLITICS/GENERAL

Dan Quayle, Bob Dole, and Bob Packwood are traveling in a car together in the Midwest. A tornado comes along, whirls them up into the air, and tosses them thousands of yards away. When they regain consciousness and extract themselves from the vehicle, they realize they're in the Land of Oz. They decide to go see the Wizard.

"I'm going to ask the Wizard for a brain," says Dan Quayle.

"I'm going to ask the Wizard for a heart," says Bob Dole.

"Where's Dorothy?" asks Bob Packwood.

WANT TO GO OUT FOR A BITE?

Rumor: C-Span is merging with the Home Shopping Network. Now we can buy our Congresspeople from the comfort of our own homes.

POLITICS / GENERAL

Q: Why do political sex scandals always seem to involve Democrats?

A: Who would risk their career for a piece of elephant?

Q: What's the difference between a dead dog lying in the road and Rush Limbaugh lying dead in the road?

A: There are skid marks in front of the dog.

Q: What's the difference between Newt Gingrich and a catfish?

A: One's a scum-sucking bottom dweller and one's a fish.

Q: What is the difference between Newt Gingrich and the *Hindenburg*?

A: One is a big fat Nazi gas bag and the other exploded in 1937.

POLITICS / GENERAL

I hear that the Democrats are considering changing their mascot from a donkey to a condom because a condom stands for inflation, halts production, discourages cooperation, protects a bunch of dicks, and gives one a sense of security while screwing others.

Q: Who was the first liberal Democrat?

A: Christopher Columbus. He left not knowing where he was going, got there not knowing where he was, left not knowing where he'd been, and did it all on borrowed money.

POLITICS / GENERAL

February 6 marked Ronald Reagan's eighty-seventh birthday. People the world over celebrated by forgetting it.

1986:

Reagan is in office and the White House purchases new china.

1996:

Clinton is in office and China purchases the White House.

POLITICS/GENERAL

Q: What's the difference between Rush Limbaugh and a whale?

A: A sportscoat!

Americans are unimpressed by the successful cloning of a sheep by Scottish scientists. They say we've been cloning sheep for years—they're known as the Christian Coalition.

Mother Teresa

...hy was baby Jesus born in a stable?
...ill Clinton is a president for our time
...This crash is just another example
f the Franco/German anti-British co
llaboration... Q: Did you hear that
he Democrats and Republicans are f
inally... Did you hear about the tri
ibute song for Mother Teresa?... W
hat did Michael Jackson say to O.J.
... Q: What's O.J. Simpson's internet
ddress?... Funny thing about the F
rank Gifford video... The top fiftee
igns your webmaster is in a cult...
ince all the the Heaven's Gates mem
embers were discovered wearing N
neakers... Q: What new sitcom is E
llen DeGeneres and Brett Butler co
ollaborating on? Q: How man
PUs does it take to turn on a li
ghtbulb?... According to the U.S. D

Q: Did you hear about the tribute song for Mother Teresa?

A: It's called "Sandal in the Wind."

Princess

Diana and Mother Teresa appear at the Pearly Gates. St. Peter says, "Tell me a little about what you did on Earth." One says, "I lived among sick and diseased people on the lowest rung of society. Every day I heard them cry out, wanting more and more of me." "Yeah," said St. Peter, "Those paparazzi are real scum. How about you, Mother Teresa?"

Q: What's the difference between Princess Di and Mother Teresa?

A: Around five days.

Q: What's the difference between Princess Di and Mother Teresa?

A: One was chaste until she died, the other was chased until she died.

Michael Jackson

Jeff Smith, public television's "Frugal Gourmet," in the face of numerous accusations of trying to seduce teenage boys, has announced his departure from the long-running series. In related news, Michael Jackson has announced the arrival of a new executive chef at his secluded Neverland Ranch...

Q: What did Michael Jackson say to O.J. Simpson?

A: I'll take care of your kids for you.

Q: What do Michael Jackson and the New York Yankees have in common?

A: They both wear one glove for no apparent reason, and they both need a twelve-year-old boy to score.

The baby was playing "Got Your Nose" with Michael, and he actually got it!

There were a lot of security guards at the hospital where Michael Jackson's wife, Debbie Rowe, was giving birth. They must have been trying to keep Michael out of the children's ward.

Q: Besides Michael and Mrs. Jackson, who is the happiest about this kid?

A: The real father.

WANT TO GO OUT FOR A BITE?

Apparently, Michael Jackson is contesting the paternity of his new son—seems the kid is half black.

A reporter interviewed Michael Jackson's wife after her pregnancy was announced and asked, "Have you been able to determine its sex?"

She answered, "No. We want to wait until after it's born."

The reporter said, "I was referring to Michael."

Knock, knock.

> Who's there?

Little Boy Blue.

> Little Boy Blue who?

Michael Jackson.

Q: Michael Jackson and Dennis Rodman were on a sinking ship. Who was saved?

A: Thousands of young boys and the NBA.

Q: What's the difference between Michael Jackson and a grocery bag?

A: One of them is white, plastic, and dangerous around young kids. The other one, you put groceries in.

Q: What'd the doctor say to Michael Jackson as he was leaving the hospital with his son?

A: Hey, only one per father!

Q: How did that woman become pregnant with Michael Jackson's baby in the first place?

A: A couple of his bodyguards dressed her up in a ten-year-old boy's outfit.

Michael Jackson is said to be interested in cloning himself instead of conceiving another child. He said it would be interesting to see what he actually looks like.

A little kid comes to his father:

Kid: Daddy, is God a man or a woman?

Dad: Both, son, God is both.

After a while the kid approaches his father again:

Kid: Daddy, is God black or white?

Dad: (after thinking for a while)
    Both, darling, both.

After a few minutes the kid comes again:

Kid: Daddy, is Michael Jackson God?

Q: Why was Michael Jackson kicked out of the Cub Scouts?

A: Because he was up to a pack a day!

Q: Why did Michael Jackson fire Boyz II Men as his opening act?

A: He thought they were a delivery service.

Knock knock.

Who's there?

Michael Jackson.

Michael Jackson who?

Good, kid! Here's twenty million bucks.

Q: Did you hear Michael Jackson is making a new Pepsi commercial?

A: He's gonna suck that kid back out of the bottle.

Q: Why are Michael Jackson's pants so small?

A: Because they aren't his!

Q: What did Michael Jackson say to Woody Allen?

A: I'll swap you a ten for two fives.

The *Star* tabloid says that Michael Jackson paid Lisa Marie Presley five million dollars not to write a tell-all book. But Lisa has already sold the story of why she married Michael in the first place— to *Unsolved Mysteries*.

WANT TO GO OUT FOR A BITE?

Q: What does Michael Jackson do in the bathtub?

A: Blow Bubbles.

O.J. Simpson

Q: Did you hear that a New York deli named a sandwich after O.J. Simpson?

A: It's full of bologna and hard to swallow, but a lot of people are buying it.

Q: What's O.J. Simpson's Internet address?

A: http-slash-slash-backslash-escape!

Q: Why were the Buffalo Bills thinking about giving O.J. Simpson another contract?

A: Because he can still cut and run.

Q: Considering the media attention the first O.J. trial gathered, where did they ever find a jury that knew nothing about O.J. for the second trial?

A: They used the first trial's jury!

Q: Did you hear that the Bills are going to retire O.J.'s number?

A: It's true. After this season, 174 Buffalo Bill will ever again wear #1783529.

WANT TO GO OUT FOR A BITE?

O.J. has a new job with Hertz—he'll be making license plates for 'em.

O.J. Simpson *cannot* be guilty of the murders he was charged with, since the two victims were stabbed to death. After all, everyone knows that Buffalo Bills *always* choke!

Two ways O.J. can raise the verdict money:

1. Spokesman for Bruno Magli shoes—"So comfortable, you forget you're wearing them."

2. Male model, since he's known to be quite a lady killer.

O.J. SIMPSON

What two things does O.J. have that every man wants?

A Heisman trophy and a dead ex-wife!

A man is on his way home from work one afternoon in L.A. He's stopped in traffic and thinks, "Wow, this traffic seems worse than usual. We're not even moving."

He notices a police officer walking down the highway in between the cars so he rolls down his window and asks, "Excuse me, officer, what's the holdup?"

"O.J. just found out the verdict of the civil trial; he's really depressed," the officer replied. "He's lying down in the middle of the highway and threatening to douse himself in gasoline and light himself on fire. He claims not to have $33.5 million for the Goldmans. I'm walking around taking up a collection for him."

The man said, "Oh really? How much have you collected so far?"

"About three hundred gallons."

Q: What's the difference between O.J. and Colonel Sanders?

A: Colonel Sanders cuts up his chicks before he batters them.

Q: What are the ingredients in the new drink called "The Simpson"?

A: O.J., a couple of slices, and a chaser.

O.J. SIMPSON

Q: Did you hear that O.J.'s eldest son is the one who killed Nicole and Ron?

A: Apparently, he went to O.J. and said, "Dad, can I borrow the Bronco?"

O.J. replied, "I dunno, go axe Nicole."

Q: What's the difference between O.J. Simpson and John Elway?

A: O.J. Simpson drives a slow, white Bronco and John Elway *is* a slow, white Bronco.

WANT TO GO OUT FOR A BITE?

The Florida Citrus Council is reportedly offering to help O.J. pay the civil verdict on the condition he changes his name to Snapple.

O.J. has signed to appear in a new Disney movie: It's called *101 Contradictions*.

O.J.'s latest alibi:
Any man who can sit
beside Howard Cosell on
Monday Night Football
without killing him
would never kill anyone.

Knock knock.

Who's there?

O.J.

O.J. who?

You're on the jury!

If an ex-football great *had* to kill his wife, why couldn't it have been Frank Gifford!?

O.J. will now be the spokesman for Starburst Fruit Chews: "The Juice Is Loose."

WANT TO GO OUT FOR A BITE?

Q: What is the difference between O.J. Simpson and Pee-wee Herman?

A: It only took twelve jerks to get O.J. off.

Q: Hey, did you hear that O.J. is starting a limo service?

A: He guarantees that he'll get you there with plenty of time to kill.

Q: What do you say to a football player in an Armani suit?

A: "Will the defendant please rise?"

John Denver

Q: Have you heard about John Denver's newest hit?

A: "Pacific Ocean Bottom"

Q: What were John Denver's last words before leaving home?

A: "I'm leaving on a jet plane, don't know when I'll be back again."

Q: What's John Denver's new song?

A: "Thank God I'm a Ocean Buoy"

Q: What forced John Denver to veer off course and spin into the bay?

A: Rocky Mountain High!

Q: Have you heard what caused the crash?

A: There were these four paparazzi in hang-gliders, you see...

John Denver was a plane down-to-earth kinda guy.

Q: What was John Denver's last hit?

A: The Pacific Ocean!

Q: How does John Denver like his drinks?

A: On the rocks.

Q: What key does John Denver sing in?

A: Sea-flat.

Q: What was John Denver smoking when he hit the water?

A: Seaweed.

Q: What were the two design flaws that plagued John Denver's experimental plane?

A: It wouldn't fly and it wouldn't float.

WANT TO GO OUT FOR A BITE?

> Apparently John Denver was about to be named the official spokesman for a beverage company. I guess Ocean Spray will have to look elsewhere now.

Q: What happened to John Denver's career in the end?

A: It took a nosedive.

Q: What is John Denver doing right now?

A: De-composing.

Here are the hits from John Denver's new album, released posthumously:

1. "Leaving on a Prop Plane"
2. "Fiberglass on My Shoulder"
3. "Windshearsong"
4. "Fishlife Concert"
5. "Back Broke Again"
6. "Cantland Express"
7. "I Don't Want to Live"
8. "One Waterworld"
9. "Poems, Prayers, and Props"
10. "Sunshine on My Window Makes Me Nosedive"

Q: What did one member of the paparazzi say to the other as John Denver took off in his plane?

A: Try to stall him.

WANT TO GO OUT FOR A BITE?

John Denver didn't take a bath before his flight, but he did wash up on shore.

Q: How did John Denver learn to fly a plane?

A: Crash course.

WANT TO GO OUT FOR A BITE?

> John Denver had an expired license. Now he is grounded permanently.

Q: What was the last thing that went through John Denver's mind before the crash?

A: The propeller.

Q: Where did John Denver spend his vacation?

A: All over Monterey Bay.

WANT TO GO OUT FOR A BITE?

John Denver's plane, *The Long-EZ,* is now called *So Long-EZ.*

Q: Why is it a tragedy that John Denver died?

A: Because he didn't have Barry Manilow with him.

Q: Did you hear that the authorities think alcohol was a factor in the crash of John Denver's plane?

A: When they got to the crash site they found J.D. on the rocks.

Last words heard on the radio before John Denver's plane went down:

"Sunshine in my eyes can make me blind."

Sports

Kathie Lee didn't really mind Frank getting caught cheating on her, but she really got pissed when she found out there was no such thing as *Tuesday Night Football*.

The funny thing about the Frank Gifford sex video is that the passes he makes now are more famous than when he was in the NFL.

SPORTS

Q: What is the difference between Cheerios and the Broncos?

A: Cheerios belong in a bowl.

WANT TO GO OUT FOR A BITE?

The L.A. Rams have a new line of cologne. It's a little different though—you wear it and someone else scores.

Q: What's the difference between the Buffalo Bills and a dollar bill?

A: You can still get four quarters out of a dollar.

Q: How many Bills players does it take to receive a kickoff?

A: Two. One to catch the ball and one to tell him to go down.

WANT TO GO OUT FOR A BITE?

A woman is picked up by Dennis Rodman in a bar. They like each other and she goes back with him to his hotel room. He removes his shirt, revealing all his tattoos, and she sees that on his arm is one that reads REEBOK. She thinks that's a bit odd and asks him about it. Dennis says, "When I play basketball, the cameras pick up the tattoo and Reebok pays me for the advertisement." A bit later, his pants are off and she sees PUMA tattooed on his leg. He gives the same explanation for the unusual tattoo. Finally, the underwear comes off and she sees the word AIDS tattooed on his Happy Man. She jumps back with shock and screams, "I'm not going to do it with a guy who has AIDS!" He says, "It's cool, baby, in a minute it's going to say ADIDAS."

Doctors say because of Michael Irvin's broken clavicle, it will be six to eight weeks before he can videotape a teammate having sex.

The Washington Bullets have changed their name so that they will no longer be associated with crime. They are now known as, simply, the Bullets.

SPORTS

Q: What do the Chicago Cubs and Pee-wee Herman have in common?

A: They both can't whack it in public!

Q: Two Dallas Cowboys were in a car. Who was driving?

A: The cops.

Q: What do you call a bunch of millionaires sitting around watching the Super Bowl?

A: The Dallas Cowboys.

A guy walks into a bar with his pet dog.

The bartender says, "No pets allowed."

The man replies, "This is a special dog. Turn on the Jets game and you'll see."

So the bartender, anxious to see what will happen, turns on the game.

The guy says, "Watch. Whenever the Jets score, my dog does flips."

The Jets keep scoring field goals and the dog keeps flipping and jumping.

"Wow! That's one hell of a dog you got there! What happens when the Jets score a touchdown?"

The man replies, "I don't know. I've only had him for seven years!"

The Dallas Cowboys adopted a new honor system: "Yes your Honor, no your Honor."

SPORTS

The Cowboys had a 12 and 4 season this year: twelve arrests, four convictions.

Q: Why is Chicago trying to sign Michael Irvin?

A: They got rid of the refrigerator, so now they want a Coke machine.

SPORTS

Q: What do you call a drug ring in Dallas?

A: A "huddle."

Q: Why are they getting rid of the artificial turf in Texas Stadium?

A: Because the Cowboys play better on grass.

WANT TO GO OUT FOR A BITE?

The Cowboys hired a new defensive coach—*Johnnie Cochran.*

Bill Gates/ Microsoft

Q: Why did Microsoft hire O.J. Simpson to announce their delivery schedules?

A: To improve their credibility.

WANT TO GO OUT FOR A BITE?

The top fifteen signs your webmaster is in a cult:

15. Every link seems to take you to www.amway.com.

14. Repetition of same banner ads: Stoli, Mott's.... Stoli, Mott's....

13. He brings twenty-three wives to the office holiday party.

12. Instead of counting up visitors, your site counts down days to the apocalypse.

11. Suddenly your travel agency's site is featuring interplanetary excursions for comet watching and one-way tickets to Guyana.

10. His home page says, "Best viewed from the Mothership."

9. Your website's "Hall of Fame" inductees are required to do a stint handing out flowers at the airport.

8. Your website is honored as the David Koresh Fan Club's "Site of the Day."

7. She has thirty-eight roommates, yet is oddly stress-free.

6. Insists that the Sabbath actually begins when *X-Files* ends.

5. Frequently mutters about the "Prophet Steve Jobs" returning to rescue the true believers.

4. Not only does he understand Unix, he *is* one.

3. Big "N" on your browser replaced by spinning head of Charles Manson.

2. He only answers to the name "Doe-bert."

1. Ugly clothes; insufficient diet; lack of sleep; goofy haircut; lives in a mansion; has many followers.... Hey, wait a minute! That's Bill Gates!!

Some angels were surprised to see Bill Gates in heaven. They wanted his autograph and couldn't think of how to approach him. So, they asked St. Peter for advice. He replied, "That's not Bill Gates, that's just God trying to be Bill Gates."

Did you hear about the woman who married three Microsoft employees and still died a virgin? Her first husband was in training, and kept teaching her how to do it herself. The second was in sales, and kept telling her how good it was going to be. And the third was in tech support, and kept saying, "Don't worry, it'll be up any minute now."

WANT TO GO OUT FOR A BITE?

Bill Gates sees Hugh Grant at a party and Divine Brown comes up in the conversation.

"I sure would like to get together with her!" says Bill.

Hugh replies, "Well, Bill, you know ever since our incident, her price has skyrocketed. She's charging a small fortune."

Bill says (with a chuckle), "Hugh, money's no object to me. What's her number?"

So Hugh gives Bill her number and Bill sets up a date. They meet and after they finish, Bill is lying there in ecstasy, mumbling, "Divine... Divine... Divine... now I know why you chose the name Divine."

To which she replies, "Thank you, Bill. And now I know why you chose the name Microsoft."

Bill Gates dies and proceeds to the pearly gates. St. Peter tells him he is a borderline case and may choose whether to go to heaven or hell. Bill asks whether he may take a look at each before deciding. He is taken to hell, where he sees joyous angels flying around and everyone is having a wonderful time. He is then taken to heaven, where he sees angels sitting about looking bored and the atmosphere is very somber.

BILL GATES/MICROSOFT

He chooses hell. On arrival he is immediately bound with barbed wire and cast into a fiery furnace. Writhing in agony, he asks Satan why he saw angels flying around and having a wonderful time when he visited hell earlier. Satan replies, "That was only the demo version!"

Q: What's the difference between Microsoft Windows and a computer virus?

A: The virus does less damage, takes up less disc space, and is easier to get rid of!

Q: How many Microsoft engineers does it take to screw in a lightbulb?

A: None. They just define Darkness™ as an industry standard.

Q: How many operating systems are required to screw in a lightbulb?

A: Just one. Microsoft is making a special version of Windows for it.

What did Bill Gates yell at his stockbroker?

"You spent my $150 million on what!? I said Snapple!"

Q: How many Apple employees does it take to screw in a lightbulb?

A: Seven. One to screw it in and six to design the T-shirts.

Q: How many Apple programmers does it take to change a lightbulb?

A: Only one, but why bother? Your light socket will just be obsolete in six months anyway.

Sometimes I wonder if Bill Gates ever has sex, or if he's satisfied enough screwing all PC users over.

A **helicopter was flying around above** Seattle when an electrical malfunction disabled all of the aircraft's electronic navigation and communications equipment. Due to the clouds and haze, the pilot could not determine the helicopter's position and was unable to steer toward the airport. The pilot saw a tall building, flew toward it, circled, drew a handwritten sign, and held it in the helicopter's window. The pilot's sign said, WHERE AM I? in large letters. People in the tall building quickly responded to the aircraft, drew a large sign, and held it in a building window. Their sign said, YOU ARE IN A HELICOPTER. The pilot smiled, waved, looked at his map, determined the course to steer to SEATAC airport, and landed safely. After they were on the ground, the copilot asked the pilot how the YOU ARE IN A HELICOPTER sign helped determine their position. The pilot responded, "I knew that had to be the Microsoft building because they gave me a technically correct, but completely useless, answer."

WANT TO GO OUT FOR A BITE?

Top nine reasons that Bill Gates would run for president:

9. He wants to buy an old Cesna, paint it flashy colors, and call it Air Force '95.

8. He heard that some government agencies were using UNIX.

7. He just thinks it would be neat to be president of two big thingies.

6. He's hot for Janet Reno.

5. His ego needs to be inflated.

4. He lost the key to his mansion, so he needs a new place to live.

3. He thinks that he can use MS Money to balance the budget.

2. He feels that Perot just didn't throw enough money at it.

1. He wants to make Windows 95 the official operating system of the United States of America.

Q: What's the difference between Bill Gates and Robert Tappen Morris Jr. (the Internet Worm Hacker)?

A: Robert Tappen Morris Jr. got six months in jail for crashing 10 percent of the computers that Bill Gates made one hundred million dollars crashing last weekend.

Q: How many Bill Gateses does it take to change a lightbulb?

A: One. He puts the bulb in and lets the world revolve around him.

Windows 95 doesn't
have any bugs,
it just develops
random features.

WANT TO GO OUT FOR A BITE?

A poor employee had been suffering dreadfully during the building of Gates's infamous new home. The unfortunate architect had used a Mac to undertake the interior and the wrath of Gates had fallen upon him. In fact, this guy was so distressed at the thought of using Windows in a design environment that he just got up one day and took his own life. He reappears at the gates of heaven where St. Peter is sitting with his clipboard. Nervously, he walks up to St. Peter. "Ah," St. Peter says, "you're the poor fellow who suffered at the hands of Gates. Don't worry, you're in heaven now. Everything is all right."

Still quivering, the poor architect says: "At last, that's wonderful. But you promise me that Bill Gates won't appear here?" St. Peter lets out a broad laugh: "Is the pope Catholic? You know what they say about rich men, needles, and camels... anyhow, we use Amigas..." Then, suddenly, beyond the pearly gates, a familiar figure appears. The poor architect falls into an apoplectic fit: "Look, look, you told me he'd never find a place in heaven, but it's him!" St. Peter turns around to see the sight. "Ah, no, my son, that's God—he just thinks he's Bill Gates..."

Anti-Microsoft slogans:

**Double your drive space:
delete Windows!**

**Ever notice how fast Windows runs?
Me neither!**

**Windows Multitasking: Screwing up
several things at once**

Windows: Just another pain in the glass

Windows NT: Windows Nice Try

**Windows: Turn your Pentium
into an XT...**

Windows: The Gates of Hell

Windows: The colorful clown suit for DOS

**Windows: So intuitive you only need
3Mb of help files**

Windows NT: Insert wallet into Drive A
and press any key to empty

Windows is for fun, OS/2 is for
getting things done

Windows 95: New look,
same multicrashing

Windows isn't a virus; viruses
actually do something

OS/2 VirusScan—"Windows found:
Remove it? [Y, N]"

Difference between a virus and Windows?
Viruses rarely fail

Time on your hands? Get Windows!

Microsoft Windows:
A virus with mouse support

Sorry, this virus requires
Microsoft Windows 3.x

A computer without Windows is like
a fish without a bicycle

Bang on the left side of your computer
to restart Windows

Bugs come in through open Windows

DOS 6.0 and Windows 3.1:
a turtle and its shell

Have you crashed your Windows today?

If Windows is user-friendly, why do you
need a 678-page manual?

Masochist: Windows programmer
with a smile

New from McAfee—WinScan:
Removes all Windows programs

The Microsoft Motto:

"We're the leaders, wait for us!"

> Fer sail cheep, Windows spel chekcer, wurks grate

BILL GATES/MICROSOFT

One of Microsoft's tech support reps was drafted and sent to boot camp. At the rifle range, he was given some instruction, a rifle, and bullets. He fired several shots at the target. The report came from the target area that all attempts had completely missed the target. The Microsoft tech rep looked at his rifle and then at the target again. He looked at the rifle again, and then at the target again. He put his finger over the end of the rifle barrel and squeezed the trigger with his other hand. The end of his finger was blown off, whereupon he yelled toward the target area: "It's leaving here just fine. The trouble must be at your end!"

Ways things would be different if Microsoft was headquartered in Southern Georgia:

1. Their number one product would be Microsoft Winders
2. Instead of an hourglass icon you'd get an empty beer bottle
3. Dialog boxes would give you the choice of "Ahh-ight" or "Naw"
4. The "Recycle Bin" in Winders 95 would be an outhouse
5. Whenever you pulled up the Sound Player you'd hear a digitized drunk redneck yelling "Freebird!"
6. Instead of "Start Me Up," the Winders 95 theme song would be "Achy-Breaky Heart"
7. PowerPoint would be named "ParPawnt"
8. Microsoft's programming tools would be "Vishul Basic" and "Vishul C++"
9. Winders 95 logo would incorporate the Confederate Flag

10. Microsoft Word would be just that: one word

11. New Shutdown WAV: "Y'all come back now!"

12. Instead of VP, Microsoft big shots would be called "Cuz"

13. Hardware could be repaired using parts from an old Trans Am

14. Microsoft Office replaced with Micr'sawft Henhouse

15. Four words: Daisy Duke Screen Saver

16. Well, the first thing you know, old Bill's a billionaire

17. Spreadsheet software would include examples to inventory dead cars in your front yard

18. Flight Simulator replaced by Tractor Pull Simulator

19. Microsoft CEO: Bubba Gates

20. Instructions for use would include "mash the control key."

Three women are sitting around talking about their husbands' performance as lovers. The first woman says, "My husband works as a marriage counselor. He always buys me flowers and candy before we make love. I like that." The second woman says, "My husband is a motorcycle mechanic. He likes to play rough and slap me around sometimes. I kinda like that." The third woman just shakes her head and says, "My husband works for Microsoft. He just sits on the edge of the bed and tells me how great it's going to be when I get it."

The Unabomber has changed tactics. It appears that explosives are no longer so frightening to his recipients, so he has found a new way to frighten people in a way that fits in with his antitechnology viewpoint. He's taken to mailing people free copies of Windows 95.

WANT TO GO OUT FOR A BITE?

If Microsoft entered the auto business:

1. New seats would require everyone to have the same butt size.

2. We'd all have to switch to Microsoft gas.

3. The U.S. government would get subsidies from an automaker—a first.

4. The oil, alternator, gas, and engine warning lights would be replaced by a single "General Car Fault" warning light.

5. Sun Motorsystems would make a car that was solar-powered, twice as reliable, five times as fast, but ran on only 5 percent of the roads.

6. You would be constantly pressured to upgrade your car.

7. You could have only one person in the car at a time, unless you bought Car 95 or CarNT—but then you would have to buy more seats.

8. Occasionally your car would die for no apparent reason and you would have to restart it. Strangely, you would just accept this as normal.

9. Every time the lines on the road were repainted, you'd have to buy a new car.

10. People would get excited about the new features of Microsoft's cars, forgetting that the same features had been available from other carmakers for years.

Windows 95 (noun): a 32-bit extension and a graphics shell for a 16-bit patch to an 8-bit operating system, originally coded for a 4-bit microprocessor, written by a 2-bit company that can't stand 1 bit of competition.

Heaven's Gate

...Why was baby Jesus born in a stable?... Bill Clinton is a president for our tim... This crash is just another example... the Franco/German anti-British co llaboration... Q: Did you hear that... e Democrats and Republicans are fi nally... Did you hear about the tri bute song for Mother Teresa?... W hat did Michael Jackson say to O.J.. ..Q: What's O.J. Simpson's Internet address?... Funny thing about the Fr ank Gifford video... The top fifteen gns your webmaster is in a cult... nce all the the Heaven's Gates mem embers were discovered wearing Ni eakers... Q: What new sitcom is E len DeGeneres and Brett Butler co llaborating on?... Q: How many D Us does it take to turn on a lig htbulb?... According to the U.S. De partment of Labor... Q: What do

Bumper Sticker:

> Too many stupid Web hackers.
>
> Not enough comets.

Since all the Heaven's Gate members were discovered wearing Nike sneakers, Nike's changing their slogan from "Just Do It" to "Maybe You Should Think About It."

It's no wonder the thirty-nine Heaven's Gate people committed suicide. You get that many people in one place working on Windows 95 and it's bound to happen!

Q: How come the Heaven's Gate guys committed suicide?

A: They didn't have the balls to live.

Q: Why did the Heaven's Gate members kill themselves?

A: Trying to keep up with the Joneses.

Q: Why did the Heaven's Gate members carry quarters in their pockets?

A: In case E.T. needed to phone home.

Q: What has seventy-eight legs, no balls, and croaks?

A: Heaven's Gate.

WANT TO GO OUT FOR A BITE?

Top ten reasons for the end of Heaven's Gate:

10. Found out the champagne wasn't Korbel.

9. Were heavily invested in Macintosh computers.

8. Found out the UFO that would take them to eternity would be serving airline food.

7. Turned off their computer before Windows 95 was completely shut down.

6. Found out the Dime-a-Minute rate was really 25 cents.

5. Baffled by simplified tax forms two weeks before filing time.

4. Realized their haircuts made them look like Sinead O'Connor.

3. Took the expiration date on their applesauce (3-26-97) too seriously.

2. Made Mr. Blackwell's Ten Worst Dressed cultists list.

1. Were using America Online for their e-mail.

When the Heaven's Gate folks were looking to get into the Web business they asked some experienced developers for advice. Most everybody they talked to said they preferred to work with UNIX. Unfortunately, nobody explained to them that this was an operating system.

Q: What did the alien say when he got to Rancho Santa Fe?

A: "Those idiots! I told them to make lots of dessert and *fill* themselves!"

Q: Did you hear about Heaven's Gate's keyboards?

A: The only two keys were Escape and Space.

Q: What do the Heaven's Gate cult and the Chicago Cubs have in common?

A: They're both dead by spring!

American Express is coming out with a credit card for cultists. The tag line will be, "Don't leave your container without it."

The coroner says they all died of asphyxiation— they couldn't get their Windows open.

Q: What does the Heaven's Gate cult have in common with a half-eaten bag of trail mix?

A: You can find lots of bananas, but no nuts.

Apparently the rationale behind the Heaven's Gate castrations was: They're computer programmers *and* they're Trekkies… they're not gonna be using 'em anyway.

Q: Did you hear that they found the last dead cult member in San Diego?

A: He was under the sink behind the Comet.

Q: Why did the thirty-nine Heaven's Gate members have rolls of quarters in their hands when they died?

A: They were prepared for Space Invaders.

Ellen DeGeneres

ABC's *Ellen* is going to have an episode this spring that's guaranteed to shock all viewers. It's going to be funny.

WANT TO GO OUT FOR A BITE?

Q: What new sitcom are Ellen DeGeneres and Brett Butler collaborating on?

A: *Grace Under Ellen.*

Ellen DeGeneres will reportedly appear on ABC's *Home Improvement* this season in an episode where Tim Allen will build the closet that she is coming out of.

WANT TO GO OUT FOR A BITE?

Q: Who is *Ellen*'s latest sponsor?

A: Snap-On Tools.

Ellen DeGeneres is building a new house. It won't have any studs, just tongue and groove.

A man is waiting for the elevator in a Hollywood office building. The elevator doors open and there stands Ellen DeGeneres and a beautiful woman. He asks, "Going down?" Ellen replies, "No, we were just talking."

High-Tech

How many Pentium designers does it take to screw in a lightbulb?

A: 1.99904274017— but that's close enough for nontechnical people.

WANT TO GO OUT FOR A BITE?

How many IBM CPUs does it take to turn on a lightbulb?

A: Thirty-three. One to process the instruction and thirty-two to process the interrupt.

HIGH-TECH

How many FORTRAN programs does it take to change a lightbulb?

A: 1.00000000001

Q: How many database engineers does it take to change a lightbulb?

A: Three: one to write the lightbulb removal program, one to write the lightbulb insertion program, and one to act as a lightbulb administrator to make sure nobody else tries to change the lightbulb at the same time.

Q: How many IBM engineers does it take to screw in a lightbulb?

A: None. They just let Marketing explain that "Dead Bulb" is a feature.

Special Computer Viruses:

Pat Buchanan Virus: Your system works fine, but it complains loudly about foreign software. Frequently accompanies the Right-to-Life and the Randall Terry virus.

Colin Powell Virus: Makes its presence known, but doesn't do anything. Secretly, you wish it would.

Hillary Clinton Virus: Files disappear, only to reappear mysteriously a year later, in another directory.

O.J. Simpson Virus: You know it's guilty of trashing your system, but you just can't prove it.

Bob Dole Virus: Could be virulent, but it's been around too long to be much of a threat.

Steve Forbes Virus: All files are reported as the same size.

Bobbitt Virus: Removes a vital part of your hard disc, then reattaches it, but that part never truly works again.

Oprah Winfrey Virus: Your 200MB hard drive suddenly shrinks to 80MB, and then slowly expands back to 200MB.

AT&T Virus: Every three minutes it tells you what great service you're getting.

Sprint Virus: Every three minutes it reminds you that you're paying too much for the AT&T virus.

Paul Revere Virus: This revolutionary virus does not horse around. It warns you of impending hard disk attack: "Once if by LAN; twice if by C."

Politically Correct Virus: Never identifies itself as a "virus," but instead refers to itself as an "electronic micro-organism."

Right-to-Life Virus: Won't allow you to delete a file, regardless of how young it is. If you attempt to erase a file, it requires you to first see a counselor about possible alternatives.

Ross Perot Virus: Activates every component in your system, just before the whole damn thing quits.

Mario Cuomo Virus: It would be a great virus, but it refuses to run.

Ted Turner Virus: Colorizes your monochrome monitor.

Arnold Schwarzenegger Virus: Terminates and stays resident. It'll be back.

Dan Quayle Virus: Their is sumthign rong with yor komputer, ewe just can't figyour outt watt!

Government Economist Virus: Nothing works, but all your diagnostic software says everything is fine.

New World Order Virus: Probably harmless, but it makes a lot of people really mad just thinking about it.

Federal Bureaucrat Virus: Divides your hard disc into hundreds of little units, each of which does practically nothing, but all of which claim to be the most important part of your computer.

Gallup Virus: Sixty percent of the PCs infected will lose 30 percent of their data 14 percent of the time (plus or minus a 3.5 percent margin of error).

Randall Terry Virus: Prints "Oh no you don't" whenever you choose (A)bort from the (A)bort, (R)etry, (F)ail message.

Texas Virus: Makes sure that it's bigger than any other file.

Adam and Eve Virus: Takes a couple bytes out of your Apple.

Congressional Virus: The computer locks up, and the screen splits in half with the same message appearing on each side of the screen. The message says that the blame for the gridlock is caused by the other side.

Airline Luggage Virus: You're in Dallas, but your data is in Singapore.

Freudian Virus: Your computer becomes obsessed with marrying its own motherboard.

PBS Virus: Your programs stop every few minutes to ask for money.

Elvis Virus: Your computer gets fat, slow, and lazy, then self-destructs, only to resurface at shopping malls and service stations across rural America.

Ollie North Virus: Causes your printer to become a paper shredder.

Nike Virus: Just does it.

Sears Virus: Your data won't appear unless you buy new cables, power supply, and a set of shocks.

Jimmy Hoffa Virus: Your programs can never be found again.

Kevorkian Virus: Helps your computer shut down as an act of mercy.

Star Trek Virus: Invades your system in places where no virus has gone before.

Health Care Virus: Tests your system for a day, finds nothing wrong, and sends you a bill for $4,500.

George Bush Virus: It starts by boldly stating, "Read my docs...no new files!" on the screen. It proceeds to fill up all the free space on your hard drive with new files, then blames it on the Congressional virus.

Cleveland Indians Virus: Makes your 486/50 machine perform like a 286AT.

Chicago Cubs Virus: Your PC makes frequent mistakes and comes in last in the reviews, but you still love it.

The Unabomber

Q: Why did the Unabomber move to the Middle East?

A: He wanted to be less conspicuous.

WANT TO GO OUT FOR A BITE?

According to the U.S. Department of Labor, over 140,000 new jobs have been created in the past few months—and that's just FBI agents in Montana.

Q: How did the Unabomber travel around the country so quickly if he hated advanced technology and liked explosions so much?

A: He took Amtrak!

Versace

Q: What was Versace's last line?

A: Chalk.

Q: Why was Versace killed?

A: He wanted Cunanan to model for him and asked for two head shots.

Q: How can you tell it's a genuine Gianni Versace blouse?

A: It has six holes but only four buttons.

Q: Why did Cunanan shoot Versace?

A: Because Gianni was wearing plaids and stripes together.

Q: What were Gianni Versace's last words?

A: "No, you can't have it with blue buttons!"

Q: How did Versace actually die?

A: He died of a heart attack when he saw that the red from his blood didn't go with the rest of his ensemble.

Q: What's the name of Gianni Versace's last shoe design?

A: 12-gauge pumps.

Q: What kind of fashion did Versace design?

A: Clothes to die for.

Q: How can you tell that Andrew Cunanan was only half the man Gianni Versace was?

A: Because it took two bullets to kill Versace.

Marv Albert

Q: Did you hear Marv Albert was complaining about the office politics at NBC?

A: He said all the backbiting he had to do was the worst!

Q: What did Marv Albert say when NBC gave him the pink slip?

A: "Thanks, already got one."

Q: What did Mike Tyson say after the Holyfield rematch?

A: "That's the last time I let Marv Albert coach me."

Q: What do Marv Albert and Mike Tyson have in common?

A: They're both from New York.

Q: Why did Marv make his girlfriend wear a baseball cap?

A: He thought she was a hat trick.

Q: What's the difference between Marv Albert and Sharon Stone?

A: Marv wears panties.

Q: Why is Marv having trouble getting a date nowadays?

A: No women want to go out with him for a bite.

Q: What do the New York Knicks and Marv's girlfriend have in common?

A: They both ended up on their backs sobbing when it was all over.

Q: Did you hear that Marv Albert is also facing a drug charge in Virginia?

A: They accused him of doing crack.

WANT TO GO OUT FOR A BITE?

New York's Marv Albert
was bored.

It had been much too long
since he'd scored.

But a hotel room tryst

surely gives a new twist

to the
"Albert Achievement Award."

Kelly Flinn

ly was baby Jesus born in a stable.
Clinton is a president for our tim
This crash is just another example
f the Franco/German anti-British co
llaboration... Q: Did you hear that
e Democrats and Republicans are fi
nally... Did you hear about the tri
ibute song for Mother Teresa?... W
hat did Michael Jackson say to O.J.
Q: What's O.J. Simpson's Internet
ddress?... Funny thing about the Fr
ank Gifford video... The top fiftee
gns your webmaster is in a cult...
nce all the the Heaven's Gates mem
embers were discovered wearing Ni
eakers... Q: What new sitcom is E
len DeGeneres and Brett Butler col
llaborating on?... Q: How many DJ
s does it take to turn on a light
ghtbulb?... According to the U.S. De
partment of Labor... Q: What do

If Kelly Flinn wanted to stay a lieutenant, she shouldn't have played with those privates.

Q: Why did Kelly Flinn join the Air Force?

A: She heard it was one big cockpit.

Lt. Kelly Flinn may have been discharged from the Air Force for adultery, but don't feel sorry for her—she was promptly offered a job flying Air Force One.

The prosecutor called Lt. Kelly Flinn a sexual predator.

Her commanding officer called her a sex addict.

The president just called her!

Mike Tyson/ Evander Holyfield

Q: What's the difference between a Metallica concert and a Tyson-Holyfield match?

A: After the Metallica concert, there's a ringing in the ears; after the bout, there are ears in the ring.

Top eighteen catchy fight sound bites:

18. Tyson-Holyfield II: The fight that was watched around the lobe.

17. It certainly was an earie fight.

16. I guess you'd call it "The bite of the century."

15. I've heard of an ear for music, but for boxing?

14. I guess Tyson bit off more than he could chew.

13. Tyson tried to win with all his bight.

12. After last night's loss to Holyfield, Tyson's going to reaffirm the expression "ear today, gone tomorrow."

11. I'm thinking of composing a "bight song" for Tyson's next bout.

10. You've heard of Friday night at the fights? In the '90s, it's Saturday night at the bites.

9. Tyson epitomizes what a prize biter is all about.

8. Tyson must have heard wrong; Holyfield said let's go out for a bite "after" the fight.

7. Tyson sure lost some edibility last night.

6. Have you noticed that Tyson chickens are missing ears?

5. Holyfield gave Tyson an earful during the fight.

4. Tyson's game plan?
   Play it by ear.

3. Tyson's favorite song?
   "The Erie Canal."

2. Tyson's favorite movie?
   From Ear to Eternity.

1. The moral of the fight? To ear is human, to forgive divine.

WANT TO GO OUT FOR A BITE?

Q: What's the difference between Evander Holyfield and corn?

A: Corn has ears!

You know what Tyson told Don King right after they got back to the dressing room?

"They're right—it *does* taste just like chicken."

Q: How many files did Evander Holyfield download from the Mike Tyson web site?

A: A couple of megabytes.

Q: What did Tyson say to Holyfield after the referee took two points away from him?

A: "Come 'ear."

Q: Have you heard that Holyfield-Tyson III is going to be held in Tennessee?

A: Yeah, Don King's calling it the Chattanooga Chew Chew.

Q: Who is Tyson's next opponent?

A: Lorena Bobbitt. Winner eats all.

If Tyson gets banned for life, he could always become a barber. Think about it: You could walk into his shop and say, "Hey, Mike! Could you take a little off the ears?"

Iron Mike will be starring in a new Nike commercial: Just Chew It!

WANT TO GO OUT FOR A BITE?

Mike's got a new title— Heavyweight Chomp of the Year.

I think Mike got it backward— he beats up his girlfriends and eats his opponents.

Q: Why did Mike Tyson learn to bite ears?

A: How else do you tell a 275-pound inmate that "no means no"?

Q: What would have made Mike Tyson's apology seem more sincere?

A: Don King drinking a glass of water at the same time!

Tyson said in the postfight interview, "I dunno what they were so excited about, in prison that's just foreplay…"

It's a good thing Holyfield did not knock Tyson to his knees.

Holyfield was asked if he intends to fight Tyson again; his reply was, "We're playin' that by ear."

Let's be thankful Tyson wasn't disqualified for biting below the belt.

I know he's an artist in the ring, but I didn't know he was Van Gogh.

WANT TO GO OUT FOR A BITE?

Holyfield was considering changing his name from Evander to Evangogh.

Holyfield/Tyson II:

If you can't beat 'em...eat 'em!

Iron Mike is a good nickname for him. After all, iron rusts and gets flaky.

Holyfield has been laughing and making light of the situation instead of going crazy, not only proving that he's a champion with good taste, but he's a champion that tastes good.

WANT TO GO OUT FOR A BITE?

I tried to look up Mike Tyson's Homepage on the Net. I was told it was removed due to not enough "hits" and too many "bytes."

It was a real
two-bit contest,
but at least
it proved
Tyson is still a
hungry fighter.

Q: What sport did Mike Tyson take up after being suspended from boxing?

A: The broad jump.

Tyson to Holyfield before the fight: "I eat punks like you for breakfast."

Holyfield's reply: "Bite me."

Mike Tyson's next fight will be against Prince Charles. Apparently, Prince Charles is the only person on the planet with ears big enough to go fifteen rounds.

Q: Why doesn't Tyson like Holyfield?

A: Something about him left a bad taste in his mouth.

WANT TO GO OUT FOR A BITE?

Apparently, Tyson mistook the boxing ring for a teething ring.